life
lived
without
me

Julionnya McCall

Printed in the United States of America
Published by Braughler Books LLC., Springboro, Ohio

First printing, 2022

ISBN: 978-1-955791-29-8
ISBN: 978-1-955791-31-1 ebook

Library of Congress Control Number: 2022906985

Ordering information: Special discounts are available on quantity purchases by bookstores, corporations, associations, and others. For details, contact the publisher at:

sales@braughlerbooks.com
or at 937-58-BOOKS

For questions or comments about this book, please write to:

info@braughlerbooks.com

Braughler™ Books
braughlerbooks.com

For my Mom Amy, and
for my Step-Dad Mark,
I love you both so much!!!

For anyone who has been hurt,
and for everyone who has
helped me through my journey.

Contents

Tears...1

Blue Silence...3

Butterflies...5

Growing Up...7

Short Seconds...9

Dancing with My Shadow...10

Loveless Love...11

Unforgiven...13

Guilty...15

Found and Left...16

Bound to Pain...16

Ran Out...16

I...17

Time...19

Something with Nothing...20

Worlds...21

Shattered...23

The 3rd...24

Realize...25

Once...27

Wish...29

Closer...30

Crime...31

Pain in Hand...33

Relations...34

Just...34

Speaking to Air...35

Glass Eyes...35

Walk Through...37

That Night...38

Mind Problems...39

Balloons...41

Imagine...42

The Pumpkins...42

Lonely...43

Scared of Loneliness...43

Frozen...44

Lights Out...45

About the Author...47

Tears

Tears ran down her face, for she is sad, sad
because she has no time, time is sad because
it has no her, and yet they love still, but
they have so many tears to spill. Time
is confronted, and she is understanding,
they still love, but even though how many
feelings where felt, she hated time, and time
hated her. She knew she would never see
the day, but she tried not to care, and when
she tried not to care, time stopped hating
her, but it was too late, she was already gone.

For time was just a number, and she was
just a girl. A girl with nothing but sadness
and time used that sadness against her.

Blue Silence

A fall from the blue skies.

A tear fell from my blue eyes.

Nobody could ever hear the silent cries.

I always fell for her toxic lies and now our love continuously dies.

Butterflies

Butterflies flying around, butterflies falling down. Catching them as if they were memories, killing them so they are no longer free. The butterflies are being born as they are being killed. There are so many only killing the bad ones because we don't want the bad memories, but without them who would we be? Butterflies flying, butterflies crying, butterflies dying.

Growing Up

When you were small people crowded around you and they acted like they had it all. You wanted to say something, you wanted to be honest and tell them the truth, so you said nothing. When you were a child, you never smiled. People pilled on you like you were worth nobodies while. You thought to yourself when and in the end, you still said nothing. When you were a teen, you were almost never seen, and when you turned sixteen everyone looked at a screen. And by the time you were an adult you had gotten many insults, you finally broke and that was the result.

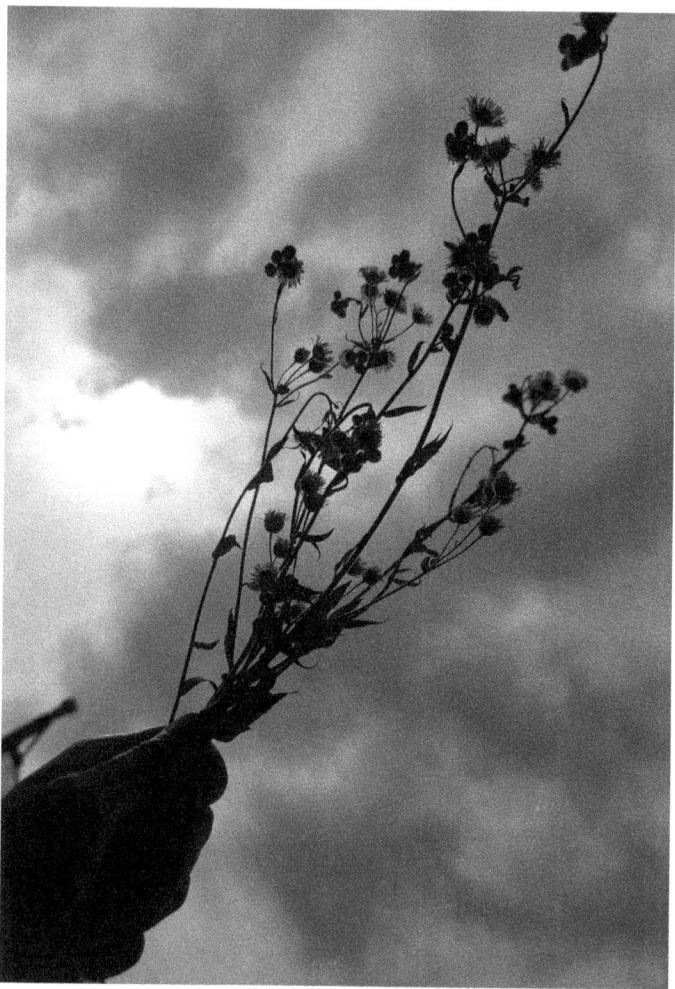

Short Seconds

They took her and I didn't care,

She screamed and I didn't hear,

Then she died and I was full of despair.

They took me and nobody cared,

I screamed, but nobody heard,

Then I died and still nobody cared.

Dancing with My Shadow

When I'm happy I'm dancing with my
shadow, but sometimes it's difficult so
were just arguing with our shadows in
hopes of a different result, but it's just
an insult to ourselves.

Loveless Love

Never in my life would I have thought
dreading not seeing you. But I did and I
do. It's like butterflies on a hot summer
day an awkwardness beyond normal
levels. Continuing with tangerines, orange
mangos, with maroon velvet colors blasting
like in the dumbest candy commercials. I
may not know if you've seen it, but it makes
me happy in a dumb way. We fell in love,
and we held on to it until we both knew we
were holding onto a loveless love.

Unforgiven

Forgiven for the crimes of breaking hearts
in which is unforgivable, but I forgive in the
presence of my pain. I forgive in the presence
of love. Not just love, but the love I had and
still have for you. But you can't love a soul-
less person. Pain shall forgive you, but love
will never forgive you.

Guilty

Incapable of truth, uncommitted
to commitment, a poison to
which kills love. Happy to be
unhappy. For this is truth spoken
by the witness. Lies spoken by the
guilty party, the guilty party of
one in which has two sides. The
witness can smell the crime in
the air, for she was the one who
witnessed treachery. The witness
speaks, for we are all fools to the
sick game guilty played. Guilty
cries for help as she has been
sentenced to karma, in which
karma does not fully punish
guilty, for guilty still has more of
her game up her sleeve. They still
longed for guilty's heart, the heart
that was covered in acid as a child.
The child never knew love and the
child is now guilty with no love.

Found and Left

People are found broken, in which making them need fixing. Then they are fixed, and in the end, they are left broken.

Bound to Pain

Therefore, broken by the force of love in which could kill rather than break, signing such contract for we are bound to pain.

Ran Out

Once upon a time, a little girl flipped a dime, she ran out of time, as if time just committed a crime.

I

Through the thick treed forest, the tree's so
tall and so green it covers the sun. therefore,
making the path without light, I walk the
path without knowing where I am going in
the darkness. I trip over many things. I get
by many things, and I fall in lots of holes.
I've lost many important things and people
along the way, but soon it turned winter
and all the leaves fell and I could see my
pathway, but it was freezing cold. I walk
barefoot in the two feet deep snow, my feet
turning purple, my body going numb, soon
falling to the ground not able to move and
being froze until I'm left with my thoughts
that continuously consume me.

Time

Listen, hear the sound of the ticking from
the pocket watch, listen, hear every second,
as the ticking speeds up faster and faster
until the ticking stopped, its gone, gone
because time flew by us.

Something with Nothing

I sit here with my head down, looking at
the water, being splashed continuously,
listening to all the noise, it's getting louder
and louder and I zone out further and
further as the noise got louder I cancel
it all out staring into the water seeing
nothing but the glow of lights reflecting
from above, sitting wondering, sitting
rethinking, sitting here trying not to
explode, more and more sound fills the
room and fills my ears, it gets too much
I use the noise cancel again, I can now
hear one sound at a time a sound of my
choice and I choose none, going deaf,
hearing nothing as nothing fills the air
as nothing fills my ears as I sit in silence
my eyes start to blur and I start to lose
sight, lose sight of the imagined noise, lose
sight of everything, soon I'm left with
my thoughts, my memories, memories of
sound and of sight, soon they all start to
fade away and I'm left here with nothing,
nothing but me, later I fade away as if I
was not there at all. Everything starting to
shut down, it all is gone and now so am I.

Worlds

We each live in our own worlds inside our
own minds yet were all in one world on
the outside, but when we fall in love it's
like two worlds are joining and becoming
one because there so in love and they
understand each other, they know when the
person there in love with needs something
or when they need comfort, they make
each other feel safe and if there worlds have
really been collided they will never fall out
of love with each other.

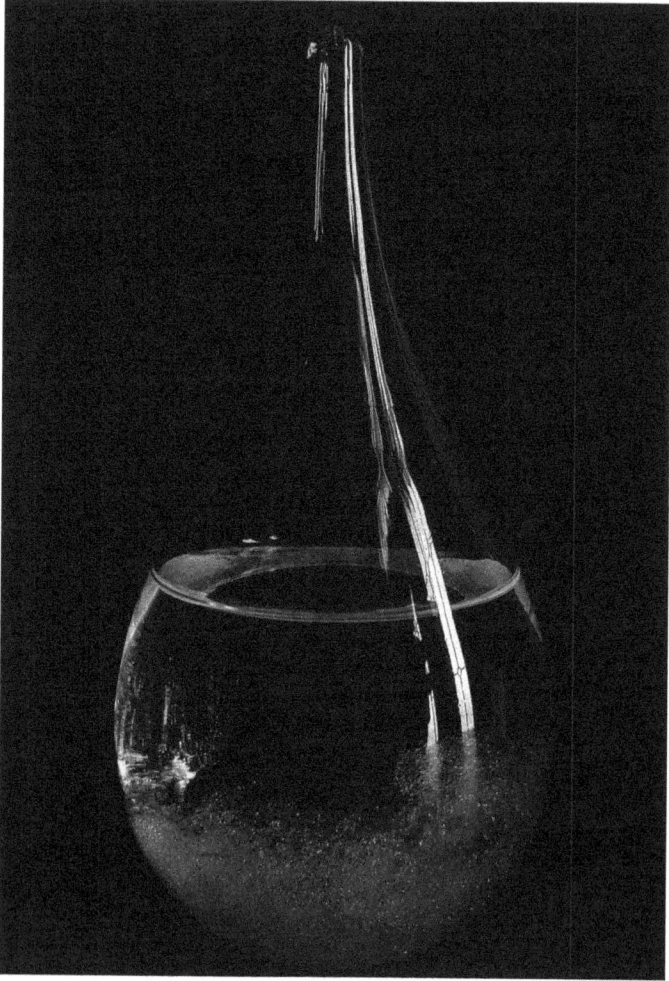

Shattered

Let the glass shatter,

let the broken pieces fall,

only to find out the broken
pieces were not broken at all.

The 3rd

She sits in the chair, and she is watching,
she is watching everyone around her live
their lives, but she is stuck in the chair. All
she can do is watch as everyone around
her go and go, yet she is with them, she is
not a part of the action, she is aside them,
continuing to watch as they continue to go,
she then realizes she is never going to be
apart; she steps forward and she falls away.
When everyone decided to look at the
girl, they have set aside it was too late she
had vanished.

Realize

She tries to hide her aggravation, and her
sadness, but she can only hide it for so long
before there comes a point in time where
she breaks, for the girl walks down the
never-ending road with many stops but
she does not know which stops are good
nor which stops are bad, but she must stop
every time at every door. For she stopped
at one door along the endless road where
in which love has been expressed, she
then becomes more visual of life, and then
moves along to the next door on the endless
road and the next door is expressing much
sadness, so she gives her feeling of love to
the door that she has stopped at, she then
realizes that love is unlimited, and giving
love is the best feeling, she then continues
her life knowing, loving, and giving, in
which at the end of her endless road she
passes on her love to someone as she goes
to the beyond and takes her long and giving
life with her to keep and remember forever.

Once

I sit alone watching the only star outside my small, tiny window, wishing it were not alone, remembering all the times I was alone until a certain someone changed it. The star is now not alone, it passes my window with a partner it is now super happy that it's not alone, its happy with all its memories of all the good time. The star had come back and now the star passes the small tint window again, but alone once more, another night passes and I see no star pass the tiny window because all the star is now is just a faded memory.

Wish

I wish I could fly,

I wish I could touch the sky,

I wish people saw what I saw in the mind,

I wish you did not leave me hanging high and dry,

So, tell me why, why did you hide?

I wonder why, you were so sly,

You just decided to lie,

Now I'm waving goodbye.

Closer

Sinking closer and closer, farther, and
farther, alive, not alive, are we alive, loving,
in love, were loving, touching hearts, our
hearts touched, simple, complicated, she,
her, you, hands clash, hands interlock, skin
burning, feelings together, alive, finally
free, watching, finally seeing, in love,
finally loving.

Crime

As if it was a crime to run out of time,

As if it was a crime to run and hide,

As if it was a crime to talk all night,

As if it was a crime to say goodbye.

Pain in Hand

I put all my pain in my hand,
then I held my hand out, and the
wind blew it away, the pain went
around in a circle and hit me in
the head, I lost my mind, then
my mind wondered back to me,
then my eyes looked at the sky
above, all the clouds ran away, all
the trees passed out, the ground
stomped and broke from under
me, I fell and I never stopped.

Relations

Love, we love, stress, our stress, hate, there
hate, regret, no regret, alive, were alive.

Just

Words are just letters, time is just numbers,
people are just alive, and stress is induced
from when everything is beginning to be
too much to handle.

Speaking to Air

No body, it's the air, we talk to the air, we
speak to the things that are not alive, it makes
us feel as if somebody actually cares, even
though they don't answer, or really listen, but
just the fact that were talking to the air makes
us feel as though that were being listened to.

Glass Eyes

Glass eyes, silent cries, I'll always tell everyone
that I'm fine, but that's ok because now time
can fly, I'll never wave goodbye, I guess for
now we must understand that not everything
works out, but in time we will find that
eventually things will be fine.

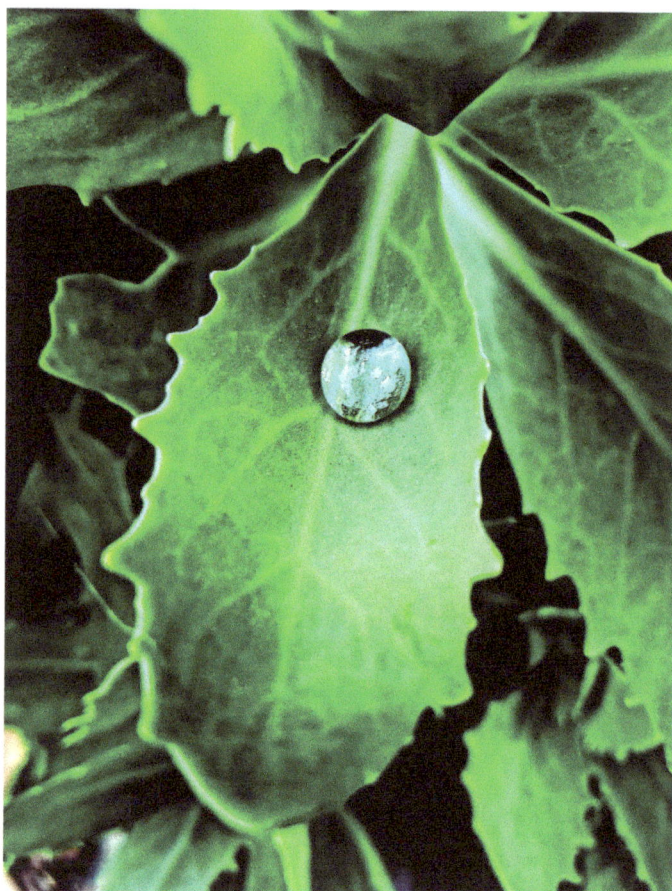

Walk Through

We're going to have to walk through this,

through the rain,

through the pain,

through everything,

we're going to have to walk through this.

That Night

I don't know what it was about that night, but the sky looked dark violet purple and I felt blue with dark and light dots floating around as if my mood was going to change to the brightest yellow of all yellows, and the trees looked dark green, and I could hear the sound of the rain hitting my black and grey umbrella, I could hear every drop of rain, I looked up and saw six lights they were dim and they looked as if they were a million miles away, I looked behind me and I could not see my shadow anymore, my umbrella has burned up to ash, I saw a single flower on the ground and it was pink and blue with a bright green stem, and then it turned blue with poky dots, then it turned yellow and then burned, I could see the fire and it turned purple, then there was nothing as if it was all a dream, but it wasn't.

Mind Problems

I look into everything, but I avoid the mirrors, it's not my fault I feel like I'm not alive. It is my fault, oh and now its knocking on the door, I told it to go away but its breaking in, and I'm powerless over it, I'm trapped now, now the pain has taken over, where am I going they can't see me I'm invisible, they will never know, they never do, soon it will be gone but no, it never leaves, it's not nice, scary thoughts are knocking at the door now, what do I do, I can't stop it from continuing to come in, I'm not having a party, get out, this is too much already, it multiplies, no, it's not fair, now my anxiety is knocking, stop screaming, no, you can't come in, the final result has let itself inside, no it can't, screaming for help, but nobody can hear my voice, leave me alone please, walking out the house, but they won't let me leave, I set fire to the house, and everything perished, I turned it off, there is no more knocking, the knocking has stopped.

Oh, a knock, walking towards the door, sinking farther into nothing, reaching for the door handle trying to escape the pull but pain, scary thoughts, anxiety, and final result is pulling me down with them, I can't escape, the house is gone, and its ashes are being pulled away by the wind as I'm being pulled away by my problems.

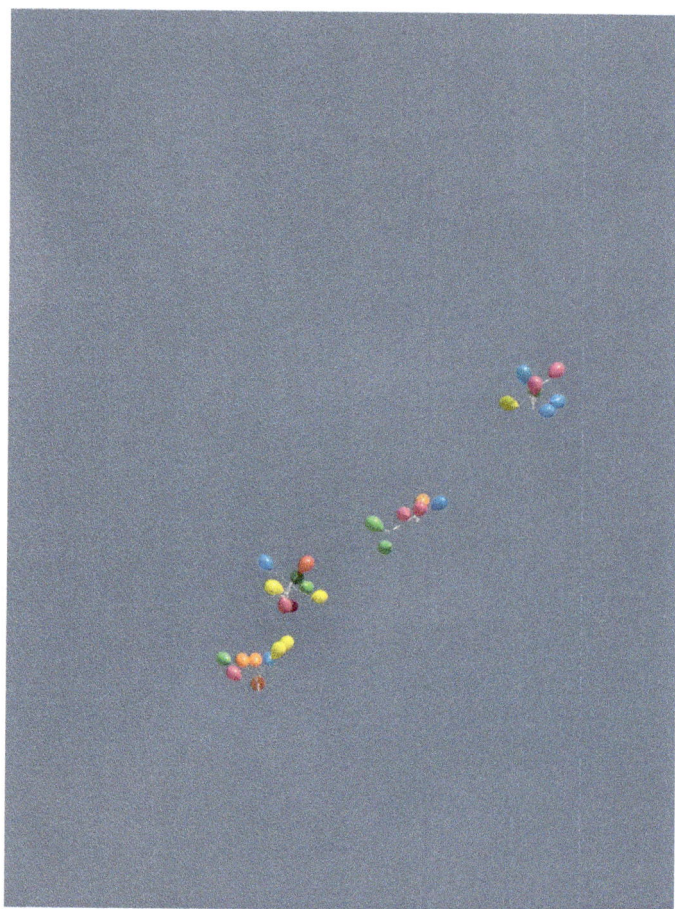

Balloons

RIP JOSÉ RICARDO GUZMAN
7/1/1988–3/2/2014

And just like that they were gone, into the wind, through the clouds, above the sun, but they shall return when the day is done, but not to us, as we would have wanted everything to go to others, and they always do.

Imagine

Surf the waves,

Walk on the moon,

Dance on the sun,

And jump among the stars.

The Pumpkins

There once were two pumpkins,

One was as big as a house,

Across the field lived one as small as a mouse,

Until the day they both faded away.

Lonely

Love is lonely without a partner,

A house is empty without people,

And our souls are bare without a soul.

Scared of Loneliness

"People are not scared of being alone,
they just want someone there to catch
them when they fall"

Frozen

I've been all up in my thoughts lately,
sleeping in the snow naked, I make it, and I
still do. I've been holding my breath longer
than I can, dipping my head in water deeper
than I can swim, and I'm still here. I feel
like I'm suffocating, getting swept up in
my feelings and yeah, I'm dealing with it.
Recently I can't catch my breath, and I don't
know what to do with it, all these excuses
I can't go through with it. I'm running
through the flames, catching the fire. All
my clothes start to burn, my skin starts to
turn and now I look like I've been through
hell. I was lead down the road too far then
I looked up and saw your heart, I know it
sounds bizarre, now I'm left all alone on
this lonely star.

Lights Out

You know it's dark when the tree's become shadows and the sun sets like cotton candy you could never have. When it's too dark you can't even see yourself in a mirror. When the sounds of bugs are telling you to sleep through the annoying sounds they make, and when everyone finally settles down and all the children cover their heads with their blankets, because the dark outside world is scary, too scary for them now. You know it's dark when the trees become shadows and your eyes start to grow tired. When you get your final glimpse of a sun setting from your view and the sky grows dark as the moon light is all you see left.

About the Author

Ever since Julionnya was a young girl, she has looked at her world as an emotionally beautiful place. Julionnya has spent the last 6 years passionately writing. She spent 13 years in a small Podunk town in Texas. Two years ago, Julionnya made the move to Ohio with her family, ready to embrace new opportunities. Julionnya is currently a high school student with many dreams for her future. When she is not studying or writing Julionnya enjoys photography, reading, talking on the phone, and eating junk food.

www.ingramcontent.com/pod-product-compliance
Lightning Source LLC
Chambersburg PA
CBHW051216150426
R18143100001BA/R181431PG42813CBX00010BA/7